# The Lost Link Recovered

FRATERNALLY DEDICATED
TO THE
## SUPREME COUNCIL OF THE THIRTY-THIRD DEGREE
OF THE
## Ancient and Accepted Scottish Rite of Freemasonry
FOR THE
Southern Jurisdiction of the United States of America.
("Mother Supreme Council of the World")
and to the Brethren of said Rite
whithersoever dispersed.

BY
**EDWIN A. SHERMAN, 33°**, Hon. Insp. Gen. Grand Cross
Past Grand Registrar and Past Grand Minister of State of the
Grand Consistory of California: Past Deputy Inspector-
General for all the Territories. Right Venerable
Grand Secretary of the Masonic Veteran
Association of the Pacific Coast.
Thirty Years.

ISBN 1-56459-443-2

Request our FREE CATALOG of over 1,000

## Rare Esoteric Books

### Unavailable Elsewhere

Alchemy, Ancient Wisdom, Astronomy, Baconian, Eastern-Thought, Egyptology, Esoteric, Freemasonry, Gnosticism, Hermetic, Magic, Metaphysics, Mysticism, Mystery Schools, Mythology, Occult, Philosophy, Psychology, Pyramids, Qabalah, Religions, Rosicrucian, Science, Spiritual, Symbolism, Tarot, Theosophy, *and many more!*

# Kessinger Publishing Company
Montana, U.S.A.

**FREDERIC II KING OF PRUSSIA.**
"(Frederic the Great.)"

(From an engraving brought from Berlin by Bro. William Nelle 32° of Oakland, Cal., in 1908, and presented to Bro. Edwin A. Sherman 33°).

"Frederic the Great" was born January 24, 1712. Initiated a Mason, August 14, 1738, at Brunswick. He was the author of the Grand Constitutions of the Ancient and Accepted Scottish Rite of Freemasonry (which included the Rite of Perfection) and signed by him on May 1st, 1786. He died August 17th, 1786.

In 1777 he sent by Bro. Baron William Frederick Auguste Steuben, his former aide-de-camp and Adjutant General, a sword to General George Washington as a token of his admiration of him as a patriot and Freemason. Fredericksburg, Virginia, was so named in his honor.

The Earl of Buchan of Scotland also sent Washington a sword.

# The Lost Link Recovered.

## THE GRAND CONSTITUTIONS OF 1786.

Our late good Brother, Albert G. Mackey 33°, a native of Charleston, South Carolina, the Moses and Lawgiver of Masonry in the United States, and the Secretary General for many years, of the Supreme Council for the Southern Jurisdiction of the United States of America, in his incomparable Encyclopedia of Freemasonry, of the "Constitutions of 1786," says as follows:

"These are regarded by the members of the Ancient and Accepted Scottish Rite as the fundamental law of their Rite. They are said to have been established by Frederick II of Prussia, in the last year of his life; a statement, however, that has been denied by some writers, and the controversies as to their authenticity have made them a subject of interest to all Masonic scholars. Brother Albert Pike, the Grand Commander of the Supreme Council for the Southern Jurisdiction of the United States, published them in 1872, in Latin, French and English; and I avail myself of his exhaustive annotations, because he has devoted to the investigation of their origin and authenticity, more elaborate care than any other writer.

"Of these Constitutions, there are two examplars, one in French and one in Latin, between which, there are, however, some material differences. For a long time the French examplar only was known in this country. It is supposed by Brother Pike, that it was brought to Charleston by Count de Grasse and that under its provisions, he organized the Supreme Council in that place. They were accepted by the Southern Supreme Council as the only authentic Constitutions. But there is abundant internal evidence of the incompleteness and incorrectness of the French Constitutions, of whose authenticity there is no proof, nor is it likely that they were made at Berlin and approved by Frederick as they profess.

"The Latin Constitutions were probably not known in France, until after the Revolution. In 1834, they were accepted as authentic by the Supreme Council of France and published in the same year. A copy of this, was published in America in 1859, by Brother Pike. These Latin Constitutions have been recently accepted (1872) by the Supreme Council of the Southern Jurisdiction in preference to the French version. Most of the other Supreme Councils—those, namely, of England and Wales, of Italy, and of South America—have adopted them as the law of the Rite, repudiating the French version as of no authority.

"The definite and well authorized conclusions to which Brother Pike has arrived on the subject of these Constitutions have been expressed by that eminent Mason in the following language:

"Said Pike: 'We think that we may safely say, that the charge that the Grand Constitutions were forged at Charleston, is completely disproved, and that it will be contemptible hereafter to repeat it. No set of speculative Jews constituted the Supreme Council established there; and those who care for the reputations of Colonel Mitchell, and Doctors Dalcho, Auld and Moultrie, may well afford to despise the scurrilous libels of the Ragons, Clavels, and Folgers.

"'And secondly, that it is not by any means *proven* or *certain* that the Constitutions were *not* really made at Berlin, as they purport to have been and approved by Frederick. We think that the preponderance of the evidence, internal and external, is on the side of their authenticity, apart from the positive evidence of the certificate of 1832.

"'And thirdly, that the Supreme Council at Charleston had a perfect right to adopt them as the law of the new Order, no matter where, when, or by whom they were made, as Anderson's Constitutions were adopted in Symbolic Masonry: that they are and always have been the law of the Rite, because they *were* so adopted; and because no man has ever lawfully received the degrees of the Rite, without swearing to maintain them as its supreme law: for as to the articles themselves, there is no substantial difference between the French and Latin copies.

"'And fourthly, that there is not one particle of *proof* of any sort, circumstantial or historical, or by argument from improbability that they are not genuine and authentic. In law, documents of great age, found in the possession of those interested under them, to whom they rightfully belong, and with whom they might naturally be expected to be found, are admitted in evidence without proof, to establish title or facts. They prove themselves, and to be avoided, must be disproved by evidence. *There is no evidence against the genuineness of these Grand Constitutions.*'"

---

For a period of forty-two years I have been an ardent and loyal supporter of these Grand Constitutions (which are to be found on the altars of the Bodies of the Rite,) both as an officer and member of the A. & A. S. Rite of Freemasonry, in the Southern Jurisdiction and on the Pacific Coast, and have aided as Deputy or charter member and officer in creating not less than thirty-five bodies of the Rite in California, Nevada and Washington, and with other brethren successfully fought its battles even against those who should have been its friends more than a third of a century ago; but truth and courage triumphed at last, *Deus Meumque Jus prevalebit.*.

Having personally enjoyed their acquaintance

# The Lost Link Recovered

and by official correspondence with Brothers Pike and Mackey, those two most eminent Masonic torch bearers of our country, from the year 1870 to the days when they were called up higher, and possessing their esteem and confidence while they lived, their memory is especially dear to me, who ere long after a life of four score years will soon follow them.

There still remains the unsettled question, however, not of the authenticity of the Grand Constitutions of 1786, but how and to whom did Frederick the Great, convey them in America to reach their destination and be found in the possession of one man who himself assumed the office of Sovereign Grand Commander, soon joined by another selected by himself, and they two organizing a new Masonic Rite with thirty-three degrees to be known as "The Ancient and Accepted Scottish Rite of Freemasonry," and they two constituting themselves as the Supreme Council on the 31st day of May, 1801, at Charleston, South Carolina.

Sir Walter Scott in "Quentin Durward," one of the Waverly Novels, in the reply made by Quentin Durward to Charles, Duke of Burgundy, when he said: "And that finally, when I did avail myself of that imputed character, it was, as if I had snatched up a shield to protect myself in a moment of emergency, and used, as I surely should have done, for the defense of myself and others, without enquiring whether I had a right to the heraldic emblazonments which it displayed."

No explanation or information was ever given by these two men, how these Constitutions came into their possession, and they have left their successors in office, and all who have sworn to maintain them as the supreme law of the Rite, in entire ignorance of the source from whom they received them. Their secret died with them, leaving that vital point of history in utter darkness.

There is a rule in geometry, that three points of any kind of a triangle being given, that the center of a circle can be found which the compass can circumscribe, that will pass through each of these three points bringing them within its radius. So in the rules of evidence, circumstantial evidence, will succeed where positive direct evidence cannot be obtained.

Evidently to my mind, it was originally the intention of Frederick the Great, that Washington himself was to be placed at the head of the new Rite in America, as he himself, was at the head of Continental Masonry in Prussia, and Louis, Prince de Bourbon in France. Frederick the Great, being the Grand Commander and the latter Lieut. Grand Commander of the Rite of Perfection of twenty-five degrees, of the Grand Consistories at Berlin and Paris.

But let us not anticipate, but investigate, by examining collateral history that will throw a side search-

**BRO. BARON FREDERICK WILLIAM AUGUSTE STEUBEN.**

The Aide de Camp and Adjutant General of the Prussian Army under "Frederic the Great."

Major General and Inspector General of the American army under Washington in the War of the Revolution for liberty and independence.

The trusted and faithful custodian of the Grand Constitutions of 1786.

Born November 15, 1730, at Magdeburg, Prussia. Was a member of the Military Lodge of the "Blazing Star" at Berlin, Prussia. Afterwards of "Trinity Lodge No. 10, now No. 12 F. & A. M. of New York City," and an honorary member of "Holland Lodge No. 8, F. & A. M." of New York City. He died November 28th, 1794, on his farm near Steubenville, Oneida County, New York. [See biographical sketch, page 9.]

light upon what was transpiring in Europe a few years antecedent to those events.

The Declaration of Liberty and Independence, gave birth to a new nation on the American continent, of the United States of America on July 4, 1776, and nearly all the active participants and promoters of the American Revolution with Washington at the head of the patriot army in the field, were Freemasons, as well as John Paul Jones of the Navy and Benjamin Franklin the United States Minister to the Court of France. As soon as the Declaration of Independence became known in Europe, volunteers in large numbers from Poland, Prussia, France and other countries, offered their services to America.

Kosciusko, Pulaski, De Kalb and others came from Poland; Lafayette with his noble devotion to the cause of American liberty threw his sword and purse into the scale accompanied by his brave countrymen from France; but for Masonic fraternal assistance to his brother George Washington, Frederick the Great, sent his most capable aid, his bosom friend and Adjutant General,

## BRO. BARON FREDERICK WILLIAM AUGUSTUS STEUBEN.

He was born November 15th, 1730, at Magdeburg, Prussia. He was educated at the colleges of Niesse and Breslau, and when only fourteen years of age, served at the siege of Prague, as a volunteer under his father. In 1747 he was appointed a cadet of infantry, and so rapid was his development in consequence, that in eleven years, when only twenty-eight years of age, he had risen to the rank of Adjutant General. He was wounded in the battle of Kunnensdorf, and in 1761, carried as a prisoner of war to St. Petersburg, but was soon after released. In the following year, he was appointed Adjutant General on the staff of Frederick the Great. Being a man of method, he was soon able to effect reforms in the Quartermaster's Department of the Prussian Army, while at the same time, he gathered together and superintended an academy for young officers, who had been selected for special military instruction.

At the close of the "Seven Years' War," he made a tour of Europe and was appointed Grand Marshal of the Prince Hohenzollern-Hackingen.

In 1777, while on a visit to Paris, he was invited by the celebrated Count St. Germain to go to America, the cause of the American Revolution being greatly favored by the French government. He at that time was a member of the "Military Lodge of the Blazing Star," at Berlin, (of which Wadzek, the Masonic writer was the orator). Having made the acquaintance of Brother Benjamin Franklin, the American Minister to the French Court, who was then popular in the salons of the elite of Paris, and after conferences with him, Baron Steuben, with his suite, sailed from Marseilles for

America in the fall of 1777, and bearing with him a sword from Frederick the Great to General George Washington, then at the head of the American Army. He arrived at Portsmouth, Virginia, December 1st, 1777, from whence he proceeded at once to the headquarters of General Washington, to whom he offered his services, which were gladly accepted. He was a thorough tactician and strategist and fully acquainted with the Prussian system. Washington and Steuben at once became fast friends.

Steuben had an income sufficient for his support, and like Lafayette and De Kalb, volunteered his services without pay or becoming a burden upon Congress. At the time of his joining the American Army, it lay encamped at Valley Forge, in a most deplorable condition. He was appointed to the office of Inspector General on May 5, 1778—his brilliant services in the Prussian Army, entitling him to the highest rank, he was commissioned a Major General. Steuben applied his ideas of military order and discipline to his new work and inaugurating important improvements in all ranks of the army; he prepared a manual of tactics, remodeled the army organization and improved its discipline; thereby bringing the American forces into a condition of much greater efficiency than they had ever before reached. He thoroughly drilled the rank and file in the manual of arms, and made them steady veterans under the fire of the enemy.

At the battle of Monmouth, Steuben as a volunteer, showed himself a thorough soldier, as he did also when in 1780, he was sent to join the army of Greene in Virginia, and at Yorktown, when he commanded in the trenches. During this siege he was on the staff of Lafayette, with whom he also was associated as a member of the Court Martial which tried and convicted Major Andre.

Steuben was remarkable for the generosity and fineness of his nature, spending his entire income, beyond what was essential to his own simple necessities, in purchasing clothing and rations for his men. He was also a most agreeable companion, possessed of a lively humor, concerning which many interesting anecdotes are related. Receiving no pay for his services during the war, and absolutely impoverishing himself for the benefit of his companions-in-arms. Congress, in 1790, voted him an annuity of $2,500, and the State of New York presented him with 16,000 acres of land in Oneida County. He built for himself a log house, at what is now known as Steubenville, divided his land among his aides and servants, and there during his last days devoted himself to his library."

Says Bro. W. J. Allen, P. M., Secretary of the Committee on Antiquities of the Grand Lodge of New York:

"Baron Steuben at the time of his death was a member of Trinity Lodge No. 10, now No. 12, and an honorary member of Holland Lodge No. 8, F. &

A. M. of New York City; and on the evening of February 6, 1789, was appointed a member of a committee to communicate to President Washington, just inaugurated President in that city, his election to honorary membership in Holland Lodge."

Baron Steuben was a member of the Dutch Reformed Church of New York.

His death on November 28th, 1794, was caused by a stroke of apoplexy, the result of his taking too little exercise. In compliance with his own request, he was wrapped in his military cloak and buried in a plain coffin without a stone to mark his grave, in the forest near by. There was then no Masonic Lodge at or near what is now Steubenville to bury his remains with Masonic honors. Afterwards on account of a road that would have run over his grave, his remains were taken up and buried not far from his farm, over which a monument was erected.

The surrender of Lord Cornwallis at Yorktown, and followed by the Treaty of Peace between the United States and Great Britain on September 3d, 1783, released the French allies who returned home to sow the seeds of "Liberty, Equality and Fraternity" and undermine and overthrow the throne of despotism, the bastiles and political prisons of France.

The United States were merely a confederation of allied autonomies with no constitution as a foundation for a permanent government, and with a possible, if not an improbable rupture, which in time, might cause them to divide into two separate nations (which three-quarters of a century afterwards was attempted, but failed after four long years of bloody war.) It was in anticipation of such a possibility that Frederick the Great in his Grand Constitutions in May 1786, provided that there might be two Supreme Councils whose Sees or seats of Government in America should be as far apart as possible from each other.

These Grand Constitutions had to be sent to a discreet brother Mason in America, whose good judgment and action at the proper moment, would insure success, and at the same time, arouse no opposition or hostility from the few scattering representatives of the Rite of Perfection of 25 degrees, wherever they might be found. The utmost circumspection and care was to be exercised in so weighty a matter, and to whom could Frederick the Great intrust this delicate mission, but to his old friend and Brother Mason, Aide de Camp and Adjutant General Baron Frederick William Steuben, the friend and Inspector General of Washington himself, and on whom but Washington did Frederick the Great desire that the office of Grand Commander of the A. & A. S. Rite should be bestowed?

On the 17th of August, 1786, Frederick the Great died, and where were these Grand Constitutions in the United States, but in the possession of Baron

Steuben, who was waiting and biding his time for the favorable opportunity to give them effect. The country was then plunged into a troubled sea of difficulty and the wisest statesmen were perplexed. John Hancock, then President of the Continental Congress, whose term expired gave way to Nathaniel Gorham of Massachusetts in 1786; he to Arthur St. Clair of Pennsylvania in 1787, and he to Cyrus Griffin of Virginia in 1788. Thus for six long years after peace was declared and ratified, was Washington and his compeers, endeavoring to straighten out the difficulty of consolidating the nation, which at last was happily effected through his efforts as President of the Convention which framed the Constitution of the United States, and declared ratified by resolution of the old Congress, September 13th, 1788. Washington was elected and inaugurated President at New York City, April 30, 1789, serving two terms and died December, 1799, aged 67 years and 10 months, and entombed at Mt. Vernon, with Masonic honors.

The field of Masonry was not then prepared for the reception of additional degrees or Rites. Dissensions and hostilities existed between the few lodges then in the country, the "Ancients" and the "Moderns," transmitted from two rival Grand Lodges of England, from whence they derived their charters, as well as jealousy of those which directly or indirectly were descended from the Grand Lodge of Scotland. The Grand Lodge of Ireland had chartered but one Lodge in America, that of "St. Patrick," Sir Wm. Johnston, as Master, (a violent tory) at Albany, New York.

There was an additional title to the A. & A. S. Rite, which it still retains. "The Royal and Military Order of the House of the Temple," which for prudent reasons was kept suppressed, for nothing then bearing the name "Royal" would have been tolerated in America.

The inventor of "The Royal Baking Powder," with his material, would have met the same fate as the tea in Boston, Annapolis and other harbors. All Masonic authority and ritualism was confined to the Blue Lodges alone, and which conferred the Royal Arch degree, but not as in England where Zerubbabel represents the king, while in America the king takes the second place, and as Dr. Oliver, the great English Masonic scholar says, "In Royal Arch Masonry, our American brethren are so imbued with republican democratic ideas, they would not tolerate the title of 'king' as the ruling officer of a Royal Arch Chapter."

The Rite of Perfection of twenty-five degrees, was introduced into the New World in 1761 by Stephen Morin in accordance with the powers with which he had been invested by the Grand Consistory of Sublime Princes of the Royal Secret, convened at Paris on the 27th of August, 1761, under the Presidency of Challon de Joinville, Substitute General of the Order.

When Morin arrived at San Domingo, agreeable to his patent and according to his instructions, he appointed Brother Moses M. Hayes as a Deputy Inspector General for North America, with the power of appointing others wherever necessary. (The office of Inspector General or Deputy Inspector General, did not include an additional degree to the 25 of the rite of Perfection). Brother Morin also appointed Brother Franckin as a Deputy Inspector General for Jamaica and the British Islands, and Brother Colonel Provost for the Windward Islands, and the British Army. The Constitutions of 1762, were transmitted to Brother Morin, soon after their adoption and ratification by the Grand Consistory of France, who furnished duly authenticated copies of the same to all the Deputy Inspector Generals appointed by him and his Deputies, and are still in force, so far as they are not modified and repealed by those of 1786.

Brother Franckin instituted a Lodge of Perfection of the Fourteenth Degree at Albany, New York, on December 20th, 1767, and conferred the degree of Sublime Prince of the Royal Secret (then the 25th degree, but now the 32,) upon a number of brethren; but this body, after its creation remained dormant for many years, and its original warrant and books of record and patents of brethren, were fifty-five years after its establishment, discovered and brought to light in 1822, by our late Brother Giles Fonda Yates. This was the first body of the Rite of Perfection planted on the continent of North America. Brother Yates by due authority revived it, and placed it under the superintendency of a Grand Council of Princes of Jerusalem, as required by the Old Constitution of 1762, and such Grand Council was subsequently opened in due form in that city.

Brother Hayes in 1781, appointed Brother Da Costa Deputy Inspector General for South Carolina, Solomon Bush for Pennsylvania and Brother Behrend Spitzer for Georgia, which appointments were confirmed by a Council of Inspectors General on the 15th of June, 1781, two years before the close of the Revolutionary War. After the death of Brother Da Costa, Brother Joseph Myers was appointed by Brother Hayes to succeed him.

Before Da Costa died, he, in accordance with the Constitutions of 1762, established a Sublime Grand Lodge of Perfection in Charleston, S. C., in 1783, where for the first time in the United States of America were the degrees from the 4th to the 14th inclusive actually worked.

On the 20th of February, 1788, a Council of Princes of Jerusalem was duly constituted at Charleston, S. C., and the officers installed by Brothers Joseph Meyers, Behrend M. Spitzer and A. Frost.

The researches into the early history of the planting of the Scottish Rite or that of Perfection in this country, prove that, notwithstanding the appointment of Inspectors Generals in the several States, the Rite was worked in Charleston, S. C., only; and to the zeal of our Charleston brethren (the most of whom were of Huguenot descent) to their constant application to the Scottish Rite, are we indebted for the foundation of the first active Bodies of the Rite in America, and the parent of all legitimate Bodies of the Scottish Rite now in existence.

But let us return to Washington and Steuben.

Soon after the beginning of the American Revolution, a disposition was manifested among American Masons to dissever their connection as subordinates with the Masonic authorities of the mother country, and in several of the newly-erected States, the Provincial Grand Lodges assumed an independent character. The idea of a Grand Master of the whole of the United States, had also become popular. On February 7th, 1780, a convention of delegates from the military lodges in the army was holden at Morristown, in New Jersey, when an address to the Grand Masters in the various States was adopted recommending the establishment of "one Grand Lodge in America," and the election of a Grand Master. This address was sent to the Grand Lodges of Massachusetts, Pennsylvania and Virginia; and although the name of Washington is not mentioned in it, those Grand Lodges were notified that he was the first choice of the brethren who had framed it.

While these proceedings were in progress, the Grand Lodge of Pennsylvania had already taken action on the same subject. On January 13th, 1780, it had held a session, and it was unanimously declared that it was for the benefit of Masonry, "that a Grand Master of Masons throughout the United States should be nominated"; whereupon with equal unanimity General Washington was elected to the office. It was then ordered that the minutes of the election be transmitted to the different Grand Lodges in the United States and their concurrence therein be requested. The Grand Lodge of Massachusetts doubted the expediency of electing a General Grand Master, declined to come to any determination on the question and so the subject was dropped.

This, said Brother Mackey, will correct the error into which many foreign Grand Lodges and Masonic writers have fallen, of supposing that Washington was ever a Grand Master of the United States.

The failure to have Washington elected Grand Master of the United States, no doubt, was the cause of Frederick the Great providing in the Grand Constitutions of 1786 for two Supreme Coun-Councils in this country and their seats of governments to be as far apart from each other as possible.

The Revolutionary War in America being over, the skeletons of an army and navy only being retained, a Constitutional Civil government to be established, all the energies and resources which Washington possessed, were devoted to his country and its interests. The organization of the Society of the Cincinnati, composed of the commissioned officers of the American army in the Revolution, was at first looked upon with disfavor, even with Washington as its President, as an attempt to create an aristocracy of military rank and a sort of nobility, while the rank and file who fought with the musket and bayonet or manned the pieces of artillery on the battlefield, were aroused to a high spirit of jealousy, when they all returned to the level of a common citizenship, and were all equal under the law without class distinction. The times were unpropitious to engraft a new Rite of European Masonry upon that of the American Blue Lodges, and whatever instructions Baron Steuben may have had from Frederick the Great, and the opportune time not arriving when he could place his trust in the hands of Washington as Grand Commander, he could only bide his time and patiently wait.

All the Inspectors and Deputy Inspectors Generals of the Rite of Perfecton in America, were foreign born, and mostly military men. Knowing that his own years were nearly numbered, and Steuben not willing that Frederick the Great's plan should utterly fail of being carried into effect, beyond a doubt, he chose his Brother Mason and Officer, Colonel John Mitchell, (a Protestant Irishman) who had served with him in the same division in the American army, and entrusted him with the duty of establishing the Ancient and Accepted Scottish Rite in accordance with the provisions of the Grand Constitutions of 1786, recommending for his aid, the son of his former fellow staff officer and also Adjutant General to Frederick the Great. That son was Dr. Frederick Dalcho, who was born in 1770, in the City of London. His father having been severely wounded, was permitted to retire to England for his health. He was a very earnest Mason and transmitted his love of Masonry to his son Frederick, who received the 33d degree as stated, from Colonel John Mitchell in 1801, and on the 31st day of May, 1801, became one of the founders of the Supreme Council of the A. & A. S. Rite and its chief exponent and historian, and located at the City of Charleston, South Carolina, and from which all regular Supreme Councils of the Rite have emanated.

If the Massachusetts Grand Lodge had concurred with that of Pennsylvania and the Convention of Delegates from the Military Lodges of the Revolutionary Army held at Morristown, New Jersey, then, no doubt, Washington being elected Grand Master of the United States of America, would also have been entrusted with the organization of the Supreme Council of the Ancient and Accepted Scottish Rite of Freemasonry of the United States of America, as its Sovereign Grand Commander, and there would never have been but one Supreme Coun-

# THE LOST LINK RECOVERED

cil at least for a century, and its Grand Lodge at the City of Washington, as is in fact that of the Southern Supreme Council, for over forty years. Massachusetts knocked out the keystone of Masonic unity of the Grand Lodges in the proposed National Arch at that time, and since then, by general consent of the craft, if so noble and self-sacrificing a patriot and Mason, who had placed his life and all upon the altar of his country, led its armies to victory, winning its liberty and independence, with the aid of his brethren in council, and in the field of war, to a triumphant peace; and as President of the Convention which drafted the Constitution, and elected and serving the first two terms under it as President of the United States, "the first in war, the first in peace, and the first in the hearts of his countrymen," if so great and good a man could not be made the Grand Master of Masons of the United States of America, then no other man should be, and this is the reason that there is no National Grand Lodge under the Stars and Stripes, our National colors, which he himself designed. This suggests the thought, that if the Grand Lodge of Massachusetts had acted concurrently with that of Pennsylvania and the Military Lodges in establishing National Masonic unity at that time, there probably in after years would have been no secession or civil war to plunge the nation into seas of blood and tears.

It no doubt had its depressing effect on Steuben and Mitchell, as well as other Masons, and that the organization of the Supreme Council must take place in a city near the most Southern limit of United States territory and that was at Charleston, South Carolina, as the most promising and desirable location that could be made. We may add here, by way of parenthesis, that it is a singular fact, that when the fanatical wave of persecutions of Masons swept over the northern portion of the United States in the early part of the last century, and the hostile anti-Masonic legislature of Massachusetts was about to pass a bill, confiscating all property belonging to Masonic bodies in that State, the Grand Lodge of Massachusetts conveyed all its property in trust, to the Grand Lodge of South Carolina, thus placing it under the protection of the United States Courts and the Federal laws.

It may not be inappropriate at this point, to quote the following from our late Ill. Bro. Giuseppe Garibaldi, 33d, of the Supreme Council of Italy, in May, 1867.

"As we have not yet a country because we have not Rome, so we have not Masonry because we are divided. I have faith that Masonic unity will draw to itself the political unity of Italy. Let them, therefore, lay aside profane passions, and conscious of the high mission entrusted to them by the noble Masonic institution, let them create the moral unity of the nation. We have not yet material unity, because moral unity is wanting. Let Masonry establish this, and that will soon be established. Brethren, I add no more. You of this sacred and unfortunate land of just attempts, will do a work truly worthy of the sons of the Vespers, if to your patriotic glories you add this other, the aureole of a moral and Masonic revolution. Let us unite and be strong, rally to conquer vice with virtue and evil with good, and the country and union will thank you.

"Masonry being the most ancient bulwark of Right and Conscience, and therefore the true antagonism of the Papacy, which is the antithesis of Progress and Civilization, I implore my brethren of all the Italian Lodges to interest themselves for us poor Romans, oppressed by the immoral domination of the bitterest enemy of Italy and Humanity."

Brother Garibaldi and Brother Victor Emmanuel of the Supreme Council of Italy lived to see their desire and this prophecy literally fulfilled.

Said the Grand Orient and Supreme Council of Portugal at that time: "Let all the Masonic bodies of the world illuminate their adepts, that they may form a grand and symbolic chain from the East to the West, and may oppose the force and union of our brethren and the sublime principles of liberty, equality and fraternity, to the shameful doctrines in the code of Jesuitism condensed in the syllabus, which can only be defended by falsehood, ignorance and the concupiscence of the satellites summoned to deliberate in the coming Ecumenical Council."

"Rome, the citadel of falsehood and intolerance, still maintains itself and defies humanity, by the *non possumus* and the Ecumenic Council, it aims to wrest from the peoples, the conquests which we have made for all alike. The heart of the Popes today that Babylon debased, sponge of all the vices, source of all iniquities. Enemy of God, it dares to war against His immutable laws. Impious Priests, preaching war and extermination aspire to envelope the peoples in the fratricidal strifes that denationalize the sacred dogma of Fraternity. The dream of the Jesuits, flattered during two centuries will be the last to be dispelled. The single flock with a single shepherd, the universal theocracy, having the Pope for chief, is in the material order, a monstrosity in presence of the progress of the free institutions of the nineteenth century, and the result of the approaching council will be the triumphant response of liberty to the last attempt of the reactionists. The temporal power will fall, and the Roman citizens freed at last from their eternal executioners, will enter into the community of free peoples. Masonry as the sanctuary of liberty, independence and justice will offer up prayers for this result; and Portuguese Masonry, in whose bosom the love of country and humanity is learned and purified, will not be the last to send up to the Supreme Architect of the Universe, supplicating prayers for the glorious triumph of the holy cause of which it is the advocate."

How faithfully have these prophecies of our Italian and Portuguese brethren been fulfilled.

# The Lost Link Recovered 27

It is well to note the principal events which occurred from the death of Frederick the Great on August 17th, 1786, to the creation of the Supreme Council at Charleston, South Carolina, May 31st, 1801, by Colonel John Mitchell and Frederick Dalcho. Brother Baron Frederick William Steuben was undoubtedly in possession of the Grand Constitutions, either at the time or shortly after the death of Frederick the Great. Steuben died of apoplexy November, 28th, 1794, aged 64 years and 13 days. Four months and two days after his death Deputy Inspector General Behrend M. Spitzer of the Rite of Perfection of 25 degrees (*not* 26), on April 2d, 1795, confers on Brother John Mitchell the Kadosh degree or the 24th of that Rite, the Illustrious Knight Commander of the Black and White Eagle, and then the 25th and highest degree of that Rite, "Most Illustrious Sovereign Prince of Masonry Grand Knight Sublime Commander of the Royal Secret," and created him a Deputy Grand Inspector General, and John Mitchell in turn on May 25th, 1801, confers the same degrees on Frederick Dalcho and creates him a Deputy Grand Inspector General of the Rite of Perfection which was under the authority of the Grand Consistory of France. But on the 31st of May, 1801, (the Revolution in France in 1798 and the years immediately following, all Masonry in that country being in a state of chaos,) these two brethren constituted themselves as the "Supreme Council of the Ancient and Accepted Scottish Rite of Freemasonry for the United States of America"; John Mitchell being in possession of the Grand Constitutions of 1786 formulated by Frederick the Great, and undoubtedly received by him from Steuben, assumes the office of Sovereign Grand Commander and appoints Frederick Dalcho Secretary General who assumes the office of the new Rite, whose father, like Steuben, had been the Aide de Camp and Adjutant General of Frederick the Great, but who had retired to London where his son Frederick was born in 1770, and upon whose death young Frederick was sent for by his uncle, who had a few years before emigrated to Baltimore.

The degrees of the two Rites were and are as follows:

### RITE OF PERFECTION.

1° Entered Apprentice. ⎫
2° Fellow Craft.             ⎬ Symbolic Lodge.
3° Master Mason.         ⎭
4° Secret Master.
5° Perfect Master.
6° Intimate Secretary.
7° Intendant of the Building.
8° Provost and Judge.
9° Elect of Nine.
10° Elect of Fifteen.
11° Illustrious Elect, Chief of the Twelve Tribes.
12° Grand Master Architect.
13° Royal Arch.
14° Grand Elect, Ancient, Perfect Master.

15° Knight of the Sword.
16° Prince of Jerusalem.
17° Knights of the East and West.
18° Rose Croix Knight.
19° Grand Pontiff.
20° Grand Patriarch.
21° Ancient Master of the Key of Masonry.
22° Prince of Libanus.
23° Sovereign Prince Adept. Chief of the Grand Consistory.
24° Illustrious Knight Commander of the Black and White Eagle.
25° Most Illustrious Sovereign Prince of Masonry. Sublime Commander of the Royal Secret.

## ANCIENT AND ACCEPTED SCOTTISH RITE.

1° Entered Apprentice.
2° Fellow Craft.
3° Master Mason.

In the United States conferred only in the Blue Lodges under the Grand Lodges' jurisdiction.

## LODGE OF PERFECTION.

4° Secret Master.
5° Perfect Master.
6° Intimate Secretary.
7° Provost and Judge.
8° Intendant of the Building.
9° Elected Knight of the Nine.
10° Illustrious Elect of the Fifteen.
11° Sublime Knights Elect of the Twelve.
12° Grand Master Architect.
13° Knight of the Ninth Arch or Royal Arch of Solomon.
14° Grand Elect, Perfect and Sublime Mason.

### COUNCIL OF PRINCES OF JERUSALEM.

15° Knight of the East.
16° Prince of Jerusalem.

### CHAPTER OF ROSE CROIX.

17° Knight of the East and West.
18° Prince of Rose Croix.

} These two bodies are now consolidated in the Southern Jurisdiction.

### COUNCIL OF KADOSH.

19° Grand Pontiff.
20° Grand Master of Symbolic Lodges.
21° *Noachite or Prussian Knight.
22° Knight of the Royal Axe or Prince of Libanus.
23° *Chief of the Tabernacle.
24° *Prince of the Tabernacle.
25° *Knight of the Brazen Serpent.
26° Prince of Mercy.
27° *Knight Commander of the Temple.
28° *Knight of the Sun or Prince Adept.
29° *Grand Scottish Knight of St. Andrew.
30° Knight Kadosh.

### CONSISTORY OF SUBLIME PRINCES OF THE ROYAL SECRET (or MASTERS OF THE KADOSH.)

31° Inspector Inquisitor Commander.
32° Sublime Prince of the Royal Secret.

### SUPREME COUNCIL.

33° *Sovereign Grand Inspector General.

---

[*The eight degrees added to the Rite of Perfection.]

## THE LOST LINK RECOVERED

Our late Brother, Albert Pike 33°, who was Sovereign Grand Commander from January 3d, 1859, until his death, April 21, 1891, declared "that there was no 33d degree until the Supreme Council was created on May 31, 1801." If there was a side or attached degree to the rank or office of Deputy Inspector General of the Rite of Perfection, then it was ignored and fell to the ground when the Supreme Council of the A. & A. S. Rite was created and it evidently was the case, for no other Inspector or Deputy Inspector General of the Rite of Perfection in the other parts of the United States were invited to be present or were present at the organization of the Supreme Council or any mention made of them. Neither Moses M. Hayes of Boston, Mass.; Behrend M. Spitzer of Georgia, nor Moses Cohen, Hyman I. Long of Philadelphia nor Alexander Francis Auguste de Grasse-Tilley, Deputy Inspector Generals of the Rite of Perfection were present on so momentous and important occasion as the organization of a new power and Rite of Freemasonry, the "Mother Supreme Council of the World."

The names of the officers and members of the Supreme Council in 1801 were Colonel John Mitchell, Sovereign Grand Commander; Dr. Frederick Dalcho, Lieutenant Grand Commander; Emanuel de la Motta, Treasurer General; Abraham Alexander, Secretary General; Major T. B. Bowen, Grand Master of Ceremonies; Israel de Lieben, Dr.

Isaac Auld, Moses C. Levy and Dr. James Moultrie, active members as Sovereign Grand Inspector Generals. Thus the Supreme Council of the Ancient and Accepted Scottish Rite of Freemasonry for the United States of America, was organized and in working order the first eight months of its existence and all of its officers and members residents of but one state and one city, with the world for its field before them.

On November 12th, 1796, four years, six months and eighteen days before the birth of the Supreme Council at Charleston, Brother Hyman Long, Deputy Inspector General of the Rite of Perfection, had created the Count de Grasse-Tilly a Deputy Inspector General of that Rite, and also issued a patent to Brother Jean Baptiste M. Delahogue and others who established under it, a grand Sublime Council of Princes of the Royal Secret at Charleston, South Carolina, January 13, 1797, confirmed by the Grand Consistory or Council at Kingston, Jamaica, but it evidently went into a state of "inocuous desuetude."

On February 21st, 1802, the Supreme Council of the A. & A. S. Rite received the Count, Brother Alexander Francis Auguste de Grasse-Tilley into its bosom, made him a member of that Supreme Council, granted him a patent of the 33d degree as Sovereign Grand Inspector General, and declared that "he was Grand Commander for life of the Supreme Council in the French West Indian Islands, made him its representative therein, and gave him power to constitute, establish, direct and inspect all Lodges, Chapters, Councils, Colleges, and Consistories of the Royal and Military Order of the Ancient and Modern Freemasonry, over the surface of the hemispheres, conformably to the Grand Constitutions."

He went to San Domingo, conferred the degrees and established bodies, but the negro insurrection drove the white population away and he left for France, where with the help of Delahogue and others on September 22d, 1804, he organized on October 20, 1804, at the City of Paris the Supreme Council of the 33d degree of the A. & A. S. Rite of Freemasonry for France, from whence in 1762 the Rite of Perfection had gone forth to the world, and on May 31st, 1801, embosomed in the A. & A. S. Rite, which bore it back to the place of its birth, which knew it not.

Ill. Brother de Grasse-Tilley 33° also established the Supreme Councils of Italy, Naples, Spain and the Netherlands in the very centers of papal hostility to free government, the rights of civil and religious liberty, and Freemasonry.

By the invasion of its territory by clandestine bodies of the Rite of Perfection the Supreme Council of the A. & A. S. Rite for the United States of America during the second war with Great Britain, which blockaded our ports, rendering travel and intercourse by sea difficult and dangerous, Brother Dr. Emmanuel de la Motta, 33°, Treasurer General, on the 5th day of August, 1813, at the city of New York, established the Supreme Council for the Northern Jurisdiction of the United States as provided for in the Grand Constitutions of 1786. This Supreme Council, whose M. P. S. Grand Commander was Brother Daniel D. Tompkins, then Vice President of the United States of America, replaced the Grand Consistory of Sublime Princes of the Royal Secret, 32d degree, which had been established by the same authority on the 6th of August, 1806. Subsequently in after years, the seat of the Northern Supreme Council was removed to Boston. Its jurisdiction embracing the States of Maine, New Hampshire, Vermont, Massachusetts, Rhode Island, Connecticut, New York, New Jersey, Pennsylvania, Ohio, Indiana, Michigan, Illinois and Wisconsin; the Southern Supreme Council retaining all the states south of these, the District of Columbia, and all the territory west of the Mississippi River acquired by treaties to the Pacific Coast, and the islands of the Pacific ocean beyond.

Up to January 3d, 1859, there had been eight Grand Commanders of the Supreme Council for the Southern Jurisdiction of the United States of America, viz.: Col. John Mitchell, May 31, 1801, to January 23, 1816; Dr. Frederick Dalcho until February 19, 1822; Dr. Isaac Auld until October 27, 1826; Dr. Moses Holbrook until December 1, 1844; Jacob de la Motta, a few weeks, when he died; Alexander McDonald until resigned, August 1,

1846; Rev. John H. Honour until he resigned, on August 13, 1858; Charles M. Furman until January 3d, 1859, when the re-incarnation of the Prophet Ezekiel took place in the person of Albert Pike, who was set down in the "Valley of Dry Bones" and they were very dry, so far as rituals and jurisprudence for the government and instruction in the propagation of the Rite was concerned. "And he said unto me, Son of man, can these bones live?" And I answered "O Lord God, thou knowest," said Albert Pike as Ezekiel.

While cogitating upon the matter as to his responsibility and duties, the cyclone of civil war swept over mountains, plains and valleys carrying him with it, and finally landed him again in the "Valley of Dry Bones," where he started from. All the prophets from Moses to Malachi responded to his call; all the philosophers from Socrates to Franklin answered his summons; Brahma, Vishnu and Siva came to his aid; Zarathustra and Mithras visited him; Osiris and Isis contributed from their stores beneath the pyramids; the cave of Elephanta emptied its treasures before him and the Oracle of Delphi telephoned in reply to his call; David, the "sweet singer of Israel," rechanted his psalms in his ears, and the "Man of Sorrows acquainted with grief," reproclaimed the law of love and the "golden rule" that he might teach it, and "John, the Beloved," made his revelation plain to his understanding; so that he heard the voice saying "Behold I make all things new, and he said unto him: Write, for these words are true and faithful," and so Albert Pike wrote the rituals anew. "And behold a shaking and the bones came together, bone to his bone: the sinews and the flesh came upon them, and the skin covered them above, but there was no breath in them, (for there was no money to pay the printer). Then said he unto Ezekiel (Pike) "Prophesy, son of man, and say to the wind. "Come from the winds, O breath, and breathe upon these slain, that they may live." So he prophesied as he was commanded, and the breath came into them (from California, Oregon, Washington, Nevada and elsewhere) and they lived and stood upon their feet, an exceeding great army (of rituals for all the jurisdictions of the Rite. English, French, Latin, Hebrew and Sanscrit were languages alike to him, and even if there had been no Grand Constitutions at all to tie to, he could have founded a new rite of Masonry entirely and established it firmly on its base, and thousands would have become its followers: for he possessed more knowledge of ancient lore, history, philosophy, poesy and variety of talent, than any man of the age in which he lived; while his magic pen from composing in his early life "The Hymns of the Gods," to his masterly anaylsis and reply to Pope Leo XIII's Papal bull of Humanum Genus, is one of the grandest declarations in defense of political and religious liberty and the rights of conscience promulgated in any age. But he held to the Grand Constitutions of 1786, the anchor of the Ancient and accepted Scottish Rite of Freemasonry, which has done so much for the uplifting of men and nations, throughout the world, and when his last hour was approaching on April 2d, 1891, he could truly say like Simeon of old, "Lord, now let thy servant depart in peace, for mine eyes have seen thy salvation," and like the Apostle Paul, "I have fought a good fight, I have finished my course. I have kept the faith." And so he went to sleep amidst his books, while his cages filled with his many companions of pet birds warbled their sweet melodies all unconscious of the departure of their loving companion and friend. To him was I especially indebted for the nomination and election to the 33d degree "as an *honorarium,* in October, 1884, for valuable services rendered in the propagation of the Rite." In fullest gratitude will his memory be cherished by me, for the honor conferred, while my time, though short, will last.

Brother Albert Pike was succeeded by Dr. James C. Batchelor as Grand Commander until his death, July 28, 1893; and he in turn by Brother Philip C. Tucker, until June 9, 1894, when he, too, was called to rest from his labors, and Brother Thomas H. Caswell, of California, became Grand Commander, whom I had known since 1849, until the day of his death, November 13, 1900, whose whole manhood in life, in Lodge, Chapter, Council, Commandery, grand and subordinate, and in the Scottish Rite for thirty years, and forty-nine years in all the service of Freemasonry and died in office. Capable, efficient and faithful to the last, his memory will be cherished most by those who loved him best. His mantle and scepter of authority fell upon one who as Grand Commander in the long line of one hundred and eight years of the existence of our Supreme Council, is second only to Albert Pike in ability, capacity, and all the qualities that make a good Grand Commander, BROTHER JAMES DANIEL RICHARDSON, judging from his addresses and allocutions delivered *ex cathedra* in the Supreme Council and other Masonic bodies, and to him we tender our most fraternal and loyal support. Long may he live to fill that high office and enjoy the esteem and love of his brethren.

It was not my intention in the preparation of this article for publication, to give a full and complete history of the Ancient and Accepted Scottish Rite, nor have I sought to do so. "Masonic tradition," so-called, cannot be satisfactorily applied to comparatively modern events, when researches will be sure to be made to ascertain the truth, as if to make a correct abstract of title to property or genealogical descent to prove a will; nor a myth take the place of fact, with men, who want to know the exact truth of the origin of things, especially where they pay their money for membership and the support of a society with which they become connected. We live in a practical age, and our fellow-men demand the reason for the faith within us, that we profess, as they have a right to do when we desire to associate them with us. To this research of more than forty years, in regard to the Grand Constitutions of 1786 of whose authenticity I have not the least doubt; and to which I have given my solemn oath of unqualified allegiance and support; though the secret died with them, whence Col. John Mitchell and Dr. Frederick Dalcho (who organized the Supreme Council of the Thirty-third Degree of the Ancient and Accepted Scottish Rite of Freemasonry at Charleston, South Carolina, on May 31, 1801,) received them; yet the circumstantial evidence is so clear to my mind, that Col. John Mitchell received them from Baron Steuben, he being unable to gain the attention and acceptance of Washington to become the Grand Commander of the Rite. Certainly Frederick the Great did not entrust them to the father of Frederick Dalcho in London where the son was born, nor could the latter in a round-about way have brought them to America, nor did Col. John Mitchell have received them direct from Frederick the Great, and started the Supreme Council on his own hook and without previous conference with some person who was near to Frederick the Great; and beyond all doubt or question in my mind, that person was the intimate and trusted friend and Brother Mason of both Frederick the Great and General George Washington, Brother Baron Frederick William Augustus Steuben, as I have given in the foregoing pages, and I believe it to be true.

If I had stated it as an absolute fact, not a scintilla of evidence could be brought forward to prove the contrary, and I submit the result of my more than forty years of research and labors to the fraternal consideration and judgment of my brethren of the Ancient and Accepted Scottish Rite, with whom I have labored so long in the sacred cause of Liberty, Equality and Fraternity.

Fraternally yours in the Mysterious Numbers,

Edwin A. Sherman, 33° Grand Cross.
1364 Franklin Stret, Oakland California, May 24th, 1909, the 60th anniversary of my arrival in California.

# The Camp of the Consistory, 32°.

Frederic the Great, to guard his own State,
Between nine of his tents, erected a fence,
Guarded by Masons to the Eighteenth Degree.
Then within the lines heptagon, he added a pentagon,
And at intervals of the five angles, within the triangles,
He placed the Mystical Standards we see.
Then an inner triangle, where nothing will dangle,
He placed in the corners the Phœnix, the Dove and the Crow.
Then within the three lines, a small circle combines,
St. Andrew's Grand Cross, long covered with moss,
When left by the traitorous and careless to grow.
But now 'tis restored, e'en by princes adored,
With none to regret, that the Royal Secret,
Within the Encampment is kept, of 1, 3, 5, 7 and 9.
For Freedom's the Word, that was carved by the Sword
Which he to Washington sent in the Name of the Lord.
Freedom of Conscience, of Speech, and of Light,
For Freemasons to Teach, and for Freemen to Fight.

## REGULATIONS

STOP WORK.
SATURDAY AFTERNOONS LAY IN XTRAS.
NOT OPEN NOR IN SUNDAYS.
TAKE EVERY NOON GAUGES & UDOMETERS.

Edwin A. Sherman, 33°, G. C.

Right Venerable Grand Secretary of the Masonic Veteran Association of the Pacific Coast.

*Sub Rosa Verbum Sapientia Sufficit.*

1364 Franklin Street, Oakland Cal.
July 4, 1908.

## The Camp of the Consistory, 32°.

"For the Lord thy God, walketh in the midst of the Camp, to deliver thee, and to give up thy enemies before thee; therefore shall thy Camp be holy; that he see no unclean thing in thee, and turn away from thee." [Deut. xxiii:14.]

"How goodly are thy tents, O Jacob, and thy tabernacles, O Israel!" [Num. xxiv:5.]